Marketing You:

Be STRATEGIC

A GOD-Centered Approach to Your Career Development

By Kimberly A. Ferguson

Marketing You: Be STRATEGIC
A God-Centered Approach to Your Career Development
ISBN-13: 978-0615948324 (Excel Service Consulting, LLC)
ISBN-10: 0615948324

Ordering Information:
Orders by U.S. trade bookstores and wholesalers. Please contact
Excel Service Consulting, LLC at 609-614-0892 or visit www.kferg.com

Permissions Information:
For permission requests, write to info@kferg.com, addressed
"Attention: Permissions Coordinator," at the address below.

Speaking Engagements:
The author, Kimberly Ferguson, is available for speaking engagements. For
speaking engagement requests, write to marketingyou@kferg.com.

Disclaimer/Message from Author:

DEDICATION

This book is dedicated to my beautiful family:

To my husband, Dewey: You always believe in me! Thank you for always pushing me and challenging me to reach my full potential. You are a wonderful husband and friend. I love you.

To my girls, Ayana and Kaci: I love you both more than you know. I am so proud to be your mommy, and so thankful to God for giving you both to me!

To my mom, Brenda: Thank you for being such an amazing force in my life. I am so grateful for your confidence in me and consistent support of me. I love you!

To the Ferguson, Highsmith, Wells, Short, McRae and Jackson families: No matter the endeavor, you always tell me how proud you are of me. It's that positivity and love that make me so grateful to be connected to each of you, and glad to be a part of our family.

CONTENTS

CHAPTER 1
INTRODUCTION

"I hate my job."

"They aren't paying me what I am worth!"

"My boss and I just don't see eye to eye."

"I need a raise."

"I'm unemployed and cannot find a job!"

"I don't feel fulfilled on this job. I need more."

"They don't respect me. My input is not valued."

"I deserve a promotion. I work hard, but it goes unnoticed. "

"I feel stuck. I want to find another job. . . but don't even know where to start."

Whether unemployed, under-employed, under-skilled, looking to change careers, or simply in search for a better opportunity, it may be time for you to consider a new approach to managing your career. Many of you will say "I've tried everything" -- career counselors, self-help books, life coaches, resume writing services, informational interviews, networking events, etc.

While I certainly agree that all of the above can be valuable resources, I have learned through first-hand observation and personal experience that the true key to career success is a God-centered approach to career management.

Wait! I am not suggesting that one can simply ask God for a job and that He will supernaturally send the opportunity your way. He is not a genie in a bottle. Although, I KNOW that He can do anything – as I've seen it happen in my own life, and in the lives of others -- in most cases, God requires you to take action as well.

Consider the following example:

My colleague, Gabby, found herself stuck in a career rut. She had been working for the same company for over 15 years, and in her position as a Senior Program Specialist for 5 years. She was a hard-worker who most of her colleagues felt deserved a promotion from Senior Program Specialist to Manager; however, her director disagreed. For reasons unknown to any of us, her director would not even entertain further conversations with Gabby regarding a promotion to management. Because I was not privy to information or interactions to which her manager was privy, I did not make a snap judgment about this situation. Instead, I was very supportive of Gabby when she shared that she had decided to begin to look outside of the department for a position with higher pay and more responsibility.

Six weeks had passed after Gabby shared her decision to move on, and I hadn't heard anything more from her on the topic. So, over lunch one afternoon I asked her if she was making any progress. Here's our conversation:

Me: *Gab, how's the hunt for a new job going?*

Gabby: *Girl, it's been tough, but I gave that thing over to God. I prayed on it and now it is in His hands.*

Me: *I know that's right. So, after you prayed, what did you do?*

Gabby: *What do you mean?*

Me: *Well, I mean, where have you applied? Have you used your connections in the company to network with the managers of other departments?*

Gabby had what I only can describe as a blank look on her face.

Me: *Ok, what about the VP of your division, didn't he invite you to an event in the city a couple of weeks ago? I heard there were many executives there. I know that had to be an awesome networking opportunity for you!*

Gabby: *No, I didn't go to that. Besides, I told you, I gave this job situation over to God. I laid my problems with this place, my boss, and my desire for a job down on the altar. And I know that God will send that opportunity my way.*

Let me qualify what you are about to read next by first saying that there is nothing wrong with having this level of faith – believing that He can and will make a way. In fact, everything is right about having Faith.

> 20 He replied, "Because you have so little faith. Truly I tell you, if you have faith as small as a mustard seed, you can say to this mountain, 'Move from here to there,' and it will move. Nothing will be impossible for you." Matthew 17:20 (NIV)

With that said, it is important that we recognize opportunity and doors opening before us. What God delivered to Gabby may not have been the actual job offer, but the opportunity to meet those people who could have given her the job of her dreams! We later found out that one of her colleagues went to the event after Gabby turned down the invitation, and ended up meeting a director on another team. A few weeks later, Gabby's colleague was offered the job that Gabby had her eye on.

I know many people will say that perhaps that opportunity wasn't for Gabby after all. "What's for me is for me", right? Well, right and wrong. If it is for you and you have the opportunity to access it, but don't take that opportunity, isn't it probable that someone else could walk through that door and access that blessing? That's not to say that the opportunity won't become available to you again at some point in the future.

We must understand that Faith is an important component to your career management strategy, but it will take more than just having faith to get to the next level.

Marketing You: Be STRATEGIC is going to provide you with real-life strategies for managing your career, built on a foundation of prayer, faith, and action. As you read through this book, think of your career as a business, and think of yourself as the CEO of that business. The key is to manage your career in a planned, deliberate way. If managed properly, every single move you make should bring you one step closer to success.

CHAPTER 2
THINKING OF A MASTER PLAN:
INTRODUCING INDIVIDUAL SUCCESS PLANS AND THE
BE STRATEGIC MODEL

Maya sat at her desk staring blankly at the screen. She had so much work to do, but could not focus. She had come to the realization weeks before that the career path she had traveled down for the past twelve years may have been the wrong one for her. Sure, working in a prestigious business organization had given her valuable experience, but it just wasn't work that she was passionate about. Now, in her mid-thirties, she was faced with the prospect of starting all over again. If this wasn't scary enough, Maya realized that she didn't know where to begin.

Ricky poured through the job search websites, desperately looking for a position for which he was qualified. A recent college graduate, he balked at the idea of having to leave his apartment and friends to move back home with his parents. He had sent out at least 50 resumes over the last two months, and had only landed two telephone interviews. Of those two telephone interviews, he was never called back for an in-person interview. He blamed his inability to find a job on the state of the economy.

Even though the above scenarios are different, there is one commonality: Maya and Ricky both need to establish a plan. They need to develop strategy to achieve their success. They need to develop their ISP. No, I am not referring to their Internet Service Provider. An ISP is an Individual Success Plan. Whether you are in a situation similar to Maya's or Ricky's, or you are in a completely different situation, you, too, must establish your Individual Success Plan (ISP).

An ISP provides a clear, detailed strategy for reaching one's goals as it relates to his/her personal definition of success. To utilize this technique, you must clearly define success – not holistically, but instead define it with an emphasis on the individual parts. The ISP simply answers the question "How will I achieve this?" for each of the individual parts of your definition of success.

What is Success? As a professional development trainer, I have used many different activities and examples to illustrate important points. Here is one example of how I used an activity to help the participants truly understand "success": One evening, I walked into the classroom and asked every adult student to draw a picture of "happiness". After getting past the bewildered and puzzled looks on some of their faces, it was quite interesting to see the different pictures that these adults drew. There were pictures of beautiful sunsets, family, children, smiles, friends, people dancing, pets, cars, money, etc. While there were many similarities amongst the pictures, each picture was notably different from the next. When the adults were asked to explain their pictures, the differences between how each person defined such a simple word were even more evident. It was clear that everyone had their own personal definition of happiness.

This same concept holds true when defining success. Each person has his/her own vision of how success should look. In order to achieve success, one must first define what success looks like to him/her. Our society would have us believe that success is defined by title, power, and money. While many may see these as crucial components to success, the key to an effective career management strategy is to figure out what success means for you. Your definition of success needs to be clear, detailed and unambiguous.

To define what success means to you, make sure you consider the importance of each of following success factors: job satisfaction, work-life balance, recognition, finances, position/title, economic status, freedom, independence, **happiness,** family. There may be other factors that you consider when defining success. Feel free to add them to your own personal map.

Job
satisfaction

Autonomy
(Independence)

Economic
status

Freedom

Success

Recognition

Happiness

Work-Life
balance

Family

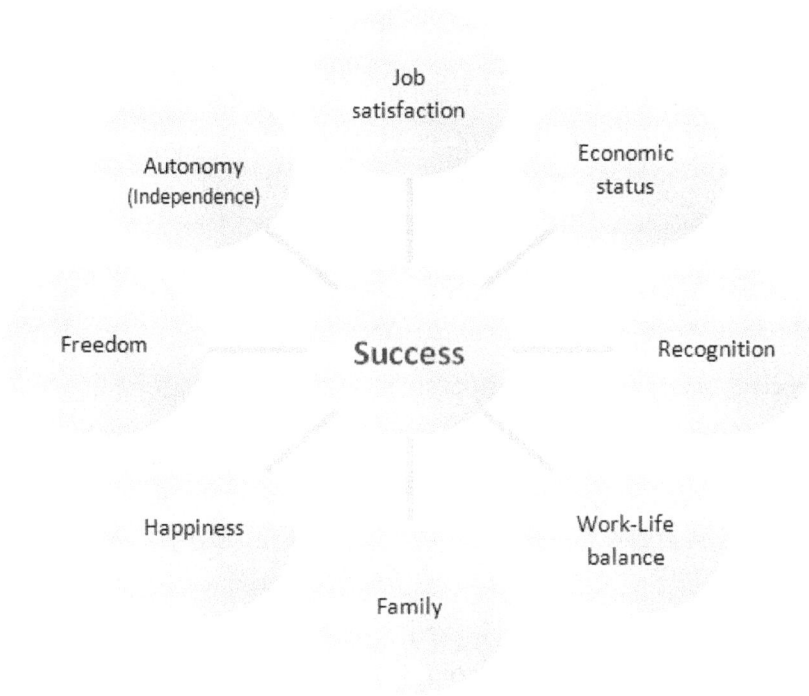

It is important to note that the aforementioned list of considerations is not all-inclusive, but it should give you a great starting point and guideline to use when defining success. Answer the question: What does success look like in terms of each of the factors? Be as specific as you can. The more detailed you are, the easier it will be for you to envision total success and create a plan to achieve that success.

Ask yourself the following questions about each Success Factor.

Success Factor:
- What does success look like in terms of {*Success Factor*}?
- How important is {*Success Factor*} to me?
- What steps will I take to achieve {*Success Factor*}?
- What can I do today to get me one step closer to {*Success Factor*}?
- What other factors are impacted by {*Success Factor*}?

To help you understand how to use this model, I've included an example of what one of my workshop participants wrote for "Job Satisfaction".

Job Satisfaction

- **What does success look like in terms of Job Satisfaction?**

  Achieving success in Job Satisfaction means that I would be satisfied and fulfilled by my job. I would be satisfied not only in my responsibilities, but I would also feel as though my values are in alignment with the culture of the organization.

- **On a scale of 1-10, how important is Job Satisfaction to me in my overall view of Success? Why?**

  Job satisfaction ranks a 9, as it is very important to me. Since I spend more time at work than I do with my family, it is very important for my health and sanity to feel satisfied and fulfilled by the job I do.

- **What steps will I take to achieve Job Satisfaction?**

  I am not currently satisfied with my job. While I am happy with the culture, my current position is not satisfying. Some steps I can take are start to research other positions in and out of the company.

- **What can I do today to get me one step closer to Job Satisfaction?**

  I can schedule a meeting with my supervisor to talk about my current role, and the possibility of taking on more responsibility.

- **What other factors are impacted by Job Satisfaction?**

  Of the factors you listed above, I would say that Job Satisfaction directly impacts overall happiness, family, and economic status/money. If I am unsatisfied with my career/work life, my overall happiness suffers. My family is also directly impacted, I noticed that on those days where I am feeling least satisfied in my career, I bring that home with me. My money is affected by my satisfaction because I am a sales representative, and I become less productive when I am not feeling satisfied. Productivity is directly related to how much I bring home!

Once you've identified what success looks like to you, it is time to map out your path to achieving that success. Remember, your ISP will answer the question of what steps you will take to make your vision of success a reality. In Chapter 6, I will cover the ISP in greater detail.

In 2009, I was working for a manager who was a true strategist. He believed in planning, planning, planning. He took pride in our successes, and he treated failure as a teachable moment. His passion for success was evident in every encounter you had with him. Our operations team spent countless hours discussing strategy for the department, which had an overall notable impact on the success of the department and organization. We set realistic goals, and developed effective plans to achieve them.

When I watched him work, I saw a genius business mind at work. He often shared anecdotes about success and quotes from other genius business minds such as Stephen Covey, Henry Ford, Ken Blanchard, etc. The most striking thing that set him apart from other managers I had worked with in the past: his belief in and dependence on God! It was refreshing to talk to someone in the business world who realized the importance of his relationship with God!

One day, while making some plans for my own personal and professional development, I noticed for the first time a parallel between some of the techniques my boss used for managing our team, and techniques I employed in my own career development, as well as the techniques that I shared with others regarding their own professional development. The similarity was two-fold:

1) *God-centered*: He had shared on numerous occasions how he had prayed over a decision; or he would quote some of the parables of Jesus to prove his point. Like my boss, I keep God at the center of my decision-making, especially when it comes to Career Development

2) *Strategic:* We both used skillful, deliberate planning to apply skillful, deliberate action.

In this chapter and the next several chapters, I will provide you with the 9 characteristics to support the Be STRATEGIC acronym, so that you can effectively incorporate these characteristics in your own career development, and develop a clear ISP.

People always asked me how I was able to land and master interviews so easily. It always came down to my dependence on the Father, and my strategy. It always came down to me being the CEO of my life!

Noticing these similarities, I went one step further, and began reading and observing how CEOs managed their businesses. I visited with my mentor who owns a multi-million dollar organization in the city. Essential to his success was planning. Like so many other successful CEOs, he does not move based on emotion. He makes decisions based on clear planning.

While I realize that this may be common-sense, the moment when I made the connection was my personal Aha! moment, and Be STRATEGIC was born. Think of your career as a business, and operate as the CEO of that business.

So, what does it mean to Be STRATEGIC? STRATEGIC is an acronym for the 9 characteristics that a successful career development plan should possess.

STRATEGIC stands for:
Self-Assessment based
Targeted
Resourceful
Action-driven and Affirmative
Tenacious
Examined or Explorative
God-centered
Integrity-guided
Conviction-powered

In the chapters that follow, we will explore this acronym. The most important of the 9 characteristics is **G**od-Centered. In Chapter 3, we will discuss this one in detail, because it is very important to remember that God must be at the center of your strategy. We need to include Him in each and every aspect of our lives --- especially our career development.

How can we ensure that God is at the center of our Career Development strategy? We can do this very simply by:

- **Praying**
- **Reading/Studying the Word**
- **Exercising our Faith**

In Chapter 5, we will explore the remaining characteristics of the Be STRATEGIC model.

The information and activities in the following chapters will also help you develop your plan, and map your way to success. I'm ready. Are you? Let's Go!

CHAPTER 3
G IS FOR GOD-CENTERED

23 Whatever you do, work it with all your heart, as working for the Lord, not for men, 24 since you know that you will receive an inheritance from the Lord as a reward. It is the Lord Jesus Christ you are serving.
Col. 3: 23-24 (NIV)

Before we can discuss any of the other characteristics associated with the STRATEGIC acronym, we must first discuss the most important. G is for God-Centered.

What does this mean? Well, very simply put, God must be at the center of everything that we do; and everything that we do must be done to His glory. This includes your career development. From the job search to your performance on the job, putting God at the core is essential.

In the previous chapter, I identified three ways that we can ensure that God is as the center of our career development strategy. It is actually quite simple. We can do this very simply by **Praying**, **Reading**, and **Exercising** (our faith).

Praying:

Jesus demonstrated for us the power and importance of Prayer. He also gave us the model prayer to show us how to communicate with God, our Father. Throughout the Word, we can see clear evidence of His prayer life.

Here are just three examples:

Situation	Supporting Scripture
To Demonstrate His Trust in God	Luke 23:46
To Make Requests	Mark 11:24
In the Face of Trouble or Distress	Mark 14:32-34

Of course, these are not the only ways, but they give a snapshot of its importance. Prayer is the method by which we can have a regular dialog with God, our Father. Our prayer time is a time that we can talk to and hear from God.

To ensure that you are consistent and effective in your prayer life, try to set aside a specific time each day that you can dedicate to spending time with God. Find a quiet space, where you can give Him uninterrupted time.

16 But Jesus often withdrew to lonely places and prayed.
Luke: 5:16 (NIV)

Why pray? We pray not only to ask him for assistance, but to thank Him for where we are right now. It is key to express thanks for your many blessings. Even if you are unemployed or under-employed, you are still blessed. Right now, take a moment to answer the following question:

> *Name five things that you can be thankful for at this very moment:*

Understanding that He is almighty and omniscient, and that He is working all things together for the good of YOU, one of His children, provides a certain level of confidence and security.

This confidence and security will be evident to all of those around you. You are a child of the Most High! You are a child of the King!

Perhaps, 1 Thessalonians 5:16-18 says it best:

16 Rejoice always, 17 pray continually, 18 give thanks in all circumstances; for this is God's will for you in Christ Jesus.
1 Thess. 5: 16-18 (NIV)

Reading/Studying the Word:

Get in the Word. Stay in the Word. Seek answers in the Word. There is nothing new under the sun, and every situation that you ever will face can be addressed and spoken to through scripture. Let God speak to you, order your steps, and guide you along your path through His Holy Written Word!

105 Your word is a lamp for my feet, a light on my path.
Psalm:119:105 (NIV)

Adopting a God-Centered approach to your career development may feel heavy. Some of you reading this may say, "I don't know where to start." There are so many resources available at our fingertips. From Study Bibles to online resources, which may identify a situation and point readers to appropriate scriptures to address those situations. Most importantly, there is your local church, where you can go to find guidance and assistance with navigating and understanding the Word's relevance in your life. If you do not have a church home, I encourage you to seek a Bible-teaching one. Every church is not for everybody, but there is a church for you.

Why read and study the Word? God's word is full of power. It speaks truth. The more you read it, the more it will speak to you and the more you will grow. The holy written word is like a seed. If we plant the seed and cultivate it, we are better positioned to reap the blessings.

Throughout this book, I talk about faith. Reading and studying is a way by which you can develop your faith. For the word tells us that faith comes by hearing the message, and the message is heard through the word!

Here are a few additional verses that answer the question "Why read?":

Reason	Scripture
We need more than bread for life	Matthew 4:4
To teach and encourage us	Romans 15:4
To prepare us for the next level	2 Timothy 3:16-17

Exercising our Faith

So, think of Faith as another muscle in the body. Even though some of us never workout, our muscles are still there; however, if we do workout, our muscles are strengthened and can do much more! It is the same way with Faith --- even if we never exercise faith, we still have a measure of faith that was given to us. But if we exercise our faith, imagine the possibilities!

So, how do we exercise our faith? We exercise our faith by
1) **Believing** and trusting in God, our Father through Jesus Christ,
2) **Participating** in a continual dialog with God through Jesus Christ by consistently praying and reading his Holy Written Word,
3) **Persevering** in the face of adversity and challenges, and not giving up.

Let's stop here at perseverance just for a moment. It is very easy for me to tell you to persevere. "Don't give up!" "See it through!" "Hang in there!" Those words of encouragement are so easy to say. But actually persevering is not that easy. In the face of challenges, sometimes it feels like it just easier to throw in the towel and quit. The bills are piling up and the bill collectors are calling; door after door appears to be closing in your face; and perhaps it feels like you can never get ahead; or maybe that is not your situation. Whatever your plight, please be encouraged in knowing that trouble and difficulty are only temporary, and you will see better days. God will bless you in the face of your difficulty and after you have seen it through. The first chapter of James speaks specifically to perseverance. Here are some specific verses that I have found to be personally helpful.

2 Consider it pure joy, my brothers and sisters, whenever you face trials of many kinds, 3 because you know that the testing of your faith produces perseverance. 4 Let perseverance finish its work so that you may be mature and complete, not lacking anything. 5 If any of you lacks wisdom, you should ask God, who gives generously to all without finding fault, and it will be given to you. James:1:2-5 (NIV)

12 Blessed is the one who perseveres under trial because, having stood the test, that person will receive the crown of life that the Lord has promised to those who love him. James 1:12 (NIV)

4)   **Taking Action** and working toward our goals

17 In the same way, faith by itself, if it is not accompanied by action, is dead. 18 But someone will say, "You have faith; I have deeds." Show me your faith without deeds, and I will show you my faith by my deeds. 19 You believe that there is one God. Good! Even the demons believe that—and shudder. James 2:17-19 (NIV)

Just like in the story I shared in Chapter 1, having Faith is wonderful, but it is essential that we put our faith to action! We must demonstrate our trust and belief in God's promises to us. But we also have to be willing to yield to the will of God. What we want may not necessarily be what God knows is best for our lives. Don't look at a closed door as God not answering your prayer; instead view that closed door as God knowing what is best for our growth and development at that stage.

If we have faith that God will provide, we must take the appropriate action to prepare for and receive His provision. For example, if I am unemployed, I can believe that an opportunity will come my way, but I have to take some level of action to ensure that I am able to receive that opportunity. Whether it is applying for jobs, networking, going on interviews, I have to put my faith to action…. And so do you!

Why exercise? Exercising our faith is just as important to our spiritual growth, as exercising our bodies is important to our physical well-being. The more we exercise our faith, the further we can reach, the higher we can go, the more we can bear. The road to career growth requires perseverance, and exercising our faith helps us prepare for the challenges, disappointments, and victories that may lie ahead.

Christiana had been unemployed for several weeks. Every morning at 7am like clockwork she jumped online to check her email, hoping to have received a response from the many employers she contacted in recent weeks. Still nothing… As she felt frustration begin to creep in, she opened her Bible to Psalm 121 (NIV):

> "1 I lift up my eyes to the mountains—
> where does my help come from?
> 2 My help comes from the Lord,
> the Maker of heaven and earth.
> 3 He will not let your foot slip—
> he who watches over you will not slumber;
> 4 indeed, he who watches over Israel
> will neither slumber nor sleep.
> 5 The Lord watches over you—
> the Lord is your shade at your right hand . . ."

"Honey," her husband interrupted, "is everything okay?"
"Yes, I'm fine." Christiana answered. "I still haven't received any calls or

emails for job interviews, but I am encouraged."

He noticed the Bible in her lap. "That's right, my love. Be encouraged. We seek strength from Him because He is the strongest. Knowing that your help comes from Him and that He has us... that is very encouraging..."

CHAPTER 4
ON FAITH: STEP OUT
MY TESTIMONY

Before we go any further with the Be STRATEGIC acronym, I think it is the appropriate time to finally share my personal testimony. In Chapter 5, I will continue to explain the remaining characteristics of the Be STRATEGIC model.

I am not sharing my testimony to boast. I am simply sharing to inspire and motivate you --- to demonstrate God's faithfulness in my life. God has been so faithful in so many areas of my life, but this testimony pertains to his faithfulness in my career development.

Part I

Fresh out of college, I took a job working for a financial publishing company. During my time there, I took advantage of various opportunities for professional growth and development. As a result, I quickly moved up and gained valuable experience in training, service, marketing, business development, and management. It was a great job with a great company, but I was not satisfied. My soul was not at rest. See, even though I was doing well (at least according to our culture's standards), I was not walking in my purpose. I had recognized my purpose early on, but life had taken me down another path. My purpose is to help others grow, develop, and achieve – through teaching and training. My gift lies in my ability to develop, implement, and deliver learning programs.
The further I went down that path, the more unsure I became about my

true purpose, the more difficult it became to see my purpose, and the more difficult it became to turn around.

The birth of a child makes you really reassess and reevaluate life! After the birth of my first daughter, I talked more and more about moving out of corporate, and finding a job in education, but the dollar signs in my eyes blurred my vision. How could I possibly take such a significant cut in pay and overall earning potential? And what if I failed? I allowed negativity and doubt to delay my blessing. Notice I said "delay"?

My husband was very supportive, and encouraged me to take the leap, but I was still hesitant. I prayed and prayed, stayed in the word, and exercised my faith, but the path was still unclear.

One cold Saturday afternoon in March, I attended an Education job fair , which didn't go exactly as I had hoped. One recruiter ripped apart my resume, questioning why someone with such a great job and diverse experience in the business world would be at an Education job fair. "What experience do you have working in a high school classroom?" she asked. Another balked "People transition from corporate because they want the summers off." I was offended, but decided not to waste my time trying to shift their thinking in the less than 5 minutes that we had together, or to defend my true reasoning for making the transition. Another recruiter presented what turned out to be the only potential opportunity --- a long-term substitute position, in which I was not at all interested.

On my ride home from the fair, I was overcome with frustration and discouragement. I realized from the feedback that I received that it could be difficult for someone like me to transition from corporate into education.

The more I reflected on the day's events, the more I questioned my decision to move into a new field. I began to talk to God – openly and honestly pouring my heart out before Him. I talked to Him until I pulled into my driveway.

Then, I sat in silence in that cold car, on that cold day. No radio, no cell phone. Silence. And as I took the time to await His answer, I heard it. The message was as clear as if someone were sitting in the seat next to me. "Step out on faith." That was it. Simple. Direct. It was at that moment that I was sure of the very steps that I needed to take.

When I went inside my house, and began to talk to my husband, he shared the exact same message with me – "Step out on faith".

That evening, I opened up the newspaper to look for job postings. There was one in particular that I was drawn to. It was a County Alternative High School. Its programs were geared toward students who did not "make it" in a traditional school setting. The majority of the children came from difficult home lives or crime-ridden communities. In addition, there were opportunities for me to provide professional development training to adults. The position was exactly what I was seeking! Purpose Realized!

I faxed my resume and cover letter that night. The very next business day, I received a call for an interview. After three interviews, and presenting a sample lesson, I was offered the job – which I gladly accepted.

Part II

After spending six years in Secondary and Higher Education, I started to get that itch again. Now, I am the type of person who needs to be challenged in the work that I do. In addition, I want to know that I'm helping others grow and develop, and making a significant impact. But this time it was more than that. It wasn't just a need to be challenged, or even to make an impact. This time the feeling was an urge, a desire to take my career to the next level, to take the knowledge and experience that I had gained during the past 16 years in order to execute purpose. I began to see those 16 years for what they were – a launching pad to catapult me to the next level.

I had incorporated my training and professional development business in 2008, but had always seen it as a "side business". And while I was consistently delivering workshops through my organization, my focus had always been my full-time employment. In 2012, the desire to grow my business grew. I continued to play with the idea of leaving my place of employment to actively work on my business, but fear of failure kept pushing me back. I was praying on it, and although I felt a tug to take the leap, I was not confident that it was in God's will for me to do so. I was allowing fear to dictate my actions.

Months passed and the desire became more intense. Developing my business was in my thoughts and was a part of every prayer. "Is this in Your will for me?" I would ask, but I wasn't receiving a clear response.

Fast Forward to March 2013. I went out with my college friend for a "Girls Night Out" in NYC and spent the night at her house. She invited me to attend her church on Sunday. I contemplated jumping back on the highway so that I could get back to my own church in time for the 12:30 afternoon service, but *SOMETHING* was pushing me to go to church with my friend.

The preacher was speaking on faith. I felt as though she was talking directly to me. Then I realized that she was. She began speaking directly to me, and directly to my situation. She said "You've been praying about that business. You've been asking God for direction. All you need to do is Step Out on Faith." I couldn't believe it. After her sermon, there was an altar call. I went up with the rest of the congregation. Before she began to pray, she walked up to me, and said "You've been praying about your business. Now, I want you to walk around it. Walk around that business. It is yours. It is yours. It is yours!"

Her words spoke to my spirit. Tears flowing down my face, I accepted each of her words, and in that moment began to take steps toward my goal. Following the Be STRATEGIC model, I began to make real and productive strides toward success.

CHAPTER 5
STRATEGIC

The STRATEGIC acronym describes the characteristics that make up a successful career development strategy. These are the characteristics that I encourage you to consider when establishing the career-related portion(s) of your individual success plan (ISP). Now it's time to examine STRATEGIC in greater detail.

Let's recap: **STRATEGIC** stands for:

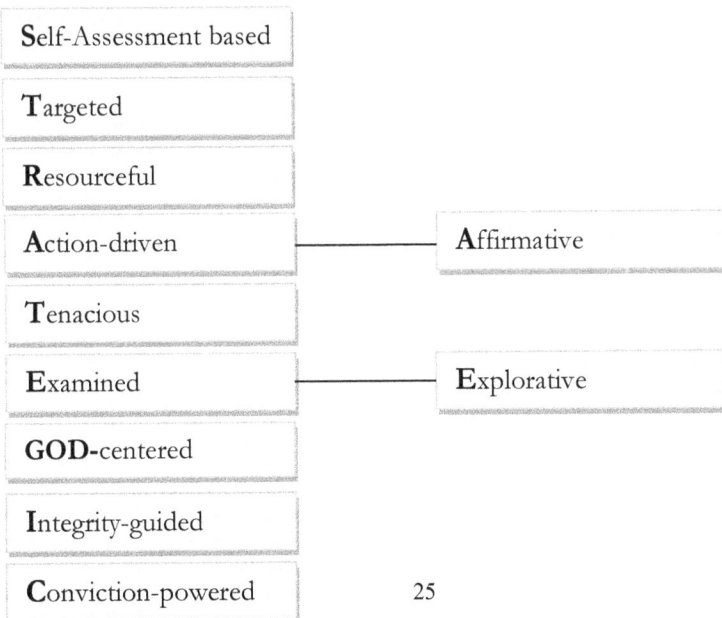

Self-Assessment based
Targeted
Resourceful
Action-driven
Tenacious
Examined
GOD-centered
Integrity-guided
Conviction-powered

Action-driven ——— **A**ffirmative

Examined ——— **E**xplorative

Please remember that the elements of the STRATEGIC model are not steps. Each element simply tells us what our career development strategy should look like. Even though the model is not a series of steps, after seeking God, Self-Assessment is very, very important.

In Chapter 3, we discussed God-centered. Over the next few pages, we will explore each of the remaining characteristics.

S is for Self-Assessment Based

We all have gifts and talents. We all have knowledge, skills, and abilities. (KSA's). It is crucial for you to understand your individual worth. It is important to recognize that God made you special, and that you have something amazing to offer. Remember, each and every one of us is a child of the King. And as His child, you are marvelous!

The key is to recognize what your gifts, talents, knowledge, skills, and abilities are, and to be able to effectively market your value throughout the career development process.

Okay, very simply put: It is important to know your value, but it is just as important to be able to positively and confidently communicate that value to others.

Self-assessment is key to your professional development. Before you can establish that plan for success, you must be clear about what you want and the value you bring. Self-assessment is about defining your value by identifying your gifts, talents, knowledge, skills, abilities, and interests. Taking an open, honest look at yourself in an effort to identify your true strengths builds confidence and establishes relevance for each career move you make!

For example: If during the self-assessment process, I determine that I have a proclivity and talent for teaching, then I can consider exploring career opportunities that allow me to satisfy this appetite and utilize this skill.

The self-assessment process is not only about your strengths. It is also key in helping you identify your weaknesses. Identifying your weaknesses will help you in the following ways:

- Help you pinpoint areas that need growth or find alternatives to using that skill
- Help you recognize what to avoid
- Help you prepare responses to interview questions, evaluation comments, etc.
- Help you develop a plan to improve on certain weaknesses

I am going to share with you two real-life examples:

I'm no artist! As a Professional Development Trainer, certain clients may ask me to storyboard an online training that I am creating for them. Storyboarding is the creation of graphic organizers to visualize one's plans for an online, interactive training module. Illustrations and images are used as part of these graphic organizers.

Well, one of my weaknesses is drawing. I am the worst at drawing pictures, diagrams, etc. I am extremely creative, and can have a great vision for how something should look in my head, but if you give me a pen and paper to illustrate that vision, watch out! What you will get from me may be a series of stick figures, shapes and unrecognizable pictures. Thank God for computers! Since I recognize my weakness, I avoid drawing. For job-related tasks that may require illustrations, I have found alternatives to drawing with a pen. Instead, I use the computer to design my diagrams and illustrations.

I'm also well prepared for interview questions associated with this skill. I focus on the fact that I can fulfill the job requirement using technology, and I highlight the benefits of that approach. Instead of identifying this as a weakness, I identified an alternative that can be sold as a benefit.

In this case, I have no plans of developing my skill of illustrating with a pen and paper. Since, I have found an alternative that works, I always use that.

This worked in this situation; however, there are other times that I have had to work at developing a weakness, as evidenced in the following example.

People love me, but I'm no social butterfly! It is hard for many to believe this --- especially those who have participated in my classes or attended my training workshops ,but I have a preference for introversion. It is hard for people who have attended my sessions to understand this because I am engaging and outgoing during my workshops. Outside of teaching, training, and facilitating, extroversion was not always easy for me. In social settings, I would sometimes feel awkward or out-of-place, primarily because socializing proved to be a bit stressful for me, when I was not among friends. I was that person who avoided lunch with my colleagues, or the person who left the company Christmas party early.

Because of what I do professionally, I identified this as a potential weakness. Within my occupation, not only do I have to teach and train, but I also have to network in order gain new clients, and maintain existing clients. I recognized the need for professional growth in this area, and began to work on it. Through reading and learning about strategies to become more effective in this area, I began to grow professionally. Another thing that I do is challenge myself to try something within this area that is productive for my professional growth each week. This may be making cold calls to potential clients, participating in a learning opportunity (webinar, training session, etc), or talking to my mentor or other professional.

In my personal examples, it is key to recognize one universal theme. Honesty. I was honest with myself concerning my strengths and weaknesses. But how does one self-assess?

In its simplest form, self-assessment can be done by asking yourself the following questions:
- What are my interests?
- What are my talents?
- About what topics am I knowledgeable?
    - How did I gain this knowledge?
        - **Education: High school, career/vocational** school, college, etc.
        - Work experience
- What are my skills/abilities?
- What are my strengths?

- What are my weaknesses?

Alternatively, you can use online and print resources. There are many sites and books dedicated to self-assessment tools and techniques, free and paid. Search online, visit a bookstore, or use your public library to find a self-assessment tool that fits your needs.

T is for Targeted

Get ready! Get set! Get focused! A focused, targeted approach to your professional development will save you time and frustration, and yield results. The "T is for Targeted" characteristic is key because it touches every area of your professional development process.

So, what is a targeted approach?

Your self-assessment, established goals, and well thought-out ISP should give you a clearer idea of the types of jobs that would best suit you. Based on this understanding, it is essential that you look for positions that are in direct alignment with your self-assessment results, goals, and action plan.

In its most basic form, a targeted approach employs research and structured keyword searches to identify and pinpoint best-fit positions for you; and tailored self-marketing techniques so that employers can easily see the value you bring.

Structured Keyword Searches: The best thing about career development in the 21st century is the availability of multiple resources at our fingertips. We can quickly search thousands of job listings in seconds, with just the click of button or the touch of a screen. But even though technology has made the search a lot easier than when I was fresh out of college, using effective technique is very important.

Once you have identified the type of position you are looking for, it is important to create a search technique that captures these positions. I encourage job seekers to learn and understand the searching capabilities of the site they're using. For example, does the site have a user friendly interface which will allow me to type in my search terms? What about complex searches: can I or should I use BOOLEAN search language when building my searches? What about parentheses and quotation marks?

The good news is that most job search sites will offer a HELP feature to assist you in building your search string. After you build an awesome search string, I suggest saving it. If the site does not allow you to save your searches, copy and paste your search into a document, so that you can easily find it, reuse it, and revise it throughout the job search process.

Tailored Self-Marketing Techniques: How do effective job seekers successfully market themselves? The answer is very simple: Differentiation. By setting yourself apart and positioning yourself as a "value-add" for a company, you can set yourself up for success. The best way to differentiate is to use tailored self-marketing.   Through tailored self-marketing, you customize any messaging that is sent to your potential employer (resume, cover letter, social networking sites, references, thank you note, and interview answers) to clearly demonstrate that you are the one for the job!

- *Resume/Cover Letter and Social Networking:* Whether you created your resume yourself, had assistance from a career professional, or hired someone to write it for you, it is absolutely imperative that you customize your resume for the job to which you are applying. It goes beyond simply personalizing the cover letter. Your resume and cover letter should clearly demonstrate why you are a good fit for the position, and show a direct correlation between the job requirements and your qualifications.

  Customizing your resume/cover letter may mean simply updating the summary of qualifications, or changing the order in which information is presented. Or, it could mean rewriting a portion of your resume and/or cover letter to better demonstrate your qualifications.

  Make sure that whatever professional experience or resume listed on social networking websites is up-to-date and consistent with professional information you are sending out via other methods.

- *References:* Select references that can speak specifically to your qualifications as they relate to the job requirements. This means that you may provide a different set of references depending on the job to which you are applying. Also, be sure to alert the references that they may be contacted, provide them with an updated copy of your resume, and a copy of the job description(s). You never want your reference to be blind-sided by a call from a potential employer.

- ***Interview Answers:*** Let your confidence shine through! Even if you hired a professional to write your resume, know your resume and be able to speak confidently about your experience and qualification. Tailor your responses to the requirements of the job, and provide real life examples of your experience. The key is to Market YOU and demonstrate the value that you bring!

- ***Thank You Note:*** The thank you note is a great way to reiterate your marketing message, follow up with your interviewer, and tie up any loose ends. You have their attention once more through the use of the thank you note. Use this opportunity wisely. Make sure that this is customized, and references something specific from the interview. Here's one specific example from my own personal experiences, in which I used the thank you note to "tie up a loose end":

> I shared earlier that I left a great corporate job to transition into the world of secondary education and professional development training. Well, in order to make that transition, I had to interview for the teaching/training position.
>
> That interview was going really well, until the principal of the school asked me to name some of the New Jersey Core Curriculum Content Standards for the subject of English. Embarrassingly, I could not name one. But, I was honest and admitted that I did not know them. Despite my honesty, he looked a bit disappointed. The rest of the interview went relatively well, and I still felt like I had a chance.
>
> As soon as I got home, I looked up the standards. Then I drafted my thank you note, in which I reiterated my interest in the position. I continued on to explain that I had downloaded and reviewed the standards as soon as I got home, and would be able to effectively incorporate them into my lesson plans. I also attached a copy of the standards.
>
> He replied, and seemed very impressed with my thank you note, and the effort I had made to recover from not knowing the answer during the interview. He offered me a second interview, during which I demonstrated clear knowledge of the standards.

In Chapter 7, we will spend some more time discussing self-marketing and personal branding.

R is for Resourceful

Another characteristic of a successful career development strategy is Resourceful --- full of resources.

As you plan your successful strategy, consider the resources to which you have access, and the resources you will need in order to reach your goals.

For the purpose of this model, our resources are people, tools, and information, as they relate to your job search and networking.

When people think about job searches, traditional resources such as newspaper want ads, popular online job boards, and employment agencies come to mind. Sure, these tools can be effective, but as you develop your career strategy, start to think outside of the box and try to reach past those traditional resources.

Network. Network. Network. First consider who you know and the connections they may have, but also be sure to consider those in your extended network. People who may be a degree or two of separation away from you may have access to the very opportunity you are looking for!

Below are three tips for ensuring that your career strategy is Resourceful: Kimberly's ABC's of Being Resourceful

- **Ask for help**: If you need assistance, ask for it.
- **Be a sponge:** Educate yourself; read books, attend workshops and webinars, and join online discussion boards to keep abreast of the trends in career development and the job market.
- **Create Opportunity:** Identify those things that you are good at, and could lead to opportunities for growth.

A is for Affirmative and Action-Driven

Affirmative

I have a friend, Brittany, who is absolutely amazing. She has a wealth of experience in her field, and is a dedicated and hard-worker. The problem? She is always doubting herself. Her confidence is lacking, and it is evident. She rarely speaks positively about herself, doesn't recognize the power and value she brings. As a result, many promotions of which she was more than qualified and deserving have passed her by over the years. This has been frustrating to her, but she never openly said or did anything about it. I've talked to her many times about her confidence, but because we are friends, I believe she has always thought I was simply being the encouraging friend.

A couple of months ago, she had an annual review. As part of the review process, she was asked to assess her own performance for the year. Then her boss would review that assessment and provide his own review of her job performance. Well, after she assessed herself, her boss, Robert called her into his office.

Before I go on, it is worth mentioning that although Brittany had been at the company for more than 15 years, her boss was relatively new to the company and had only been her manager for about 15 months.

Brittany entered his office, and he asked her to take a seat. A copy of her self-assessment lay in front of her. Their conversation went something like this:

Robert: *I just reviewed your self-assessment, Brittany. And, I have to say that I am a little disappointed. I'm going to have to ask you to redo the assessment, and resubmit it to me.*

Brittany: *Umm, ok. Can you tell me why? Is there something in particular that I overstated?*

Robert: *That is just the problem, Brittany. You understated everything. Since I've been with the company, I have found you to be such a valuable asset, yet you rate your performance as average or "needs improvement. I took a look at your previous years' reviews, and you have always given yourself low grades. I had often wondered why you were not in a higher paying position, but* *this explains it! If you don't give yourself a vote of confidence, others won't. If you don't see the value you bring, how can you expect others to?*

At that moment, Brittany understood. With guidance and support, she re-wrote her self-review. Since then, she has created a development plan, and she is well on her way to a promotion and higher paying position.

Affirmative is another important characteristic. Throughout your career development, you have to be able to positively and confidently communicate your knowledge, skills, abilities, value, etc. There are many techniques that people use to become more affirmative. Some may include:

- ***Reading daily affirmations:*** There are many resources that you can find online (free and paid) and in bookstores. Many believe that reading daily affirmations are healing to one's mind, body, and spirit.

- ***Listening to affirmation audio/Watching affirmation video:*** When I was in high school, my friend's father used to listen to positive affirmations in his car. I remember whenever he would pick us up from school, the cassette tapes would be playing in his car: "You are a strong person. You are a valuable asset to your family and workplace. You are an intelligent person. You are a skilled decision-maker". At the time, as a high school student, I didn't understand the power of hearing those positive messages, but now I believe in the power of positive affirmative messaging to build a more positive perception of oneself and a more positive approach to life.

  Just like the printed affirmation, both audio and video resources are at your fingertips. Just use your preferred search engine to find free and paid tools online.

  • ***Reciting Affirmations:*** This is definitely my favorite of the three techniques, because it is a more personalized approach and incorporates one's self-assessment results. I'm also a fan of this one because of its power. There is power in what we say. What we speak can result in consequences --- positive or negative. I would prefer to speak positivity into my life. Wouldn't you?

Check out Proverbs 18:20-21.

20 From the fruit of their mouth a person's stomach is filled; with the harvest of their lips they are satisfied. 21 The tongue has the power of life and death, and those who love it will eat its fruit.
(Proverbs 18:20-21 NIV)

In this approach one recites a list of affirmations that are relevant to his/her life on a regular schedule. On the following page, I will describe a technique that I have used, and that has proven effective for me.

Once again, there are many resources that can teach you step-by-step how to create, recite, and meditate upon your affirmations. Find the technique that works best for you and implement it in your life!

Positive Affirmations

Kimberly's A³ Technique
Assess Affirm Act

o Consider your positive attributes, and make an inventory of your best qualities as they relate to your career.

o Consider your goals and/or the negative self-perceptions you wish to change.

o In relationship to the above positive attributes and goals, make a list of positive statements.
- Start statements related to your current status with: "I am",
- Start statements related to future goals with "I can" or "I will".
The statements can only be positive and cannot be negative.
Create at least 25 statements. Here are some examples:

- I am an expert in my field.
- I am a valuable asset to my department.
- I can manage a project successfully.
- I can lead our team to success.
- I will complete this project on time and under budget.
- I will become the project manager for our largest client.

o After creating your statements, put the statements related to future goals in order of priority.

o Establish a regular routine for reciting and/or meditating on these statements. It is important to say the words, but it is more important to think about what these words mean in relationship to your development.

o Do not forget! Leave yourself reminders and post them where you can see them (on the refrigerator, on your bathroom mirror).

o Update them. Make a practice of writing new affirmations! As you recognize new things about yourself, develop new "I am" statements. As you accomplish your goals, update your "I can" and "I will".

Action-Driven

A is also for Action-Driven. Now, I know I have addressed this point a number of times throughout this book; however, it is a point worth reiterating. A well-planned career development strategy cannot sit on your faith alone. A well-planned career development strategy must be executed. Faith by itself is dead. Action is imperative.

> 14 What good is it, my brothers and sisters, if someone claims to have faith but has no deeds? Can such faith save them? 15 Suppose a brother or a sister is without clothes and daily food. 16 If one of you says to them, "Go in peace; keep warm and well fed," but does nothing about their physical needs, what good is it? 17 In the same way, faith by itself, if it is not accompanied by action, is dead. James 2:14-17 (NIV):

T is for Tenacious

Never give up! When I was a child in the Youth Choir at my church, we sang a song "I Don't Feel No Ways Tired". This song can be applied to any tribulation we face; however for the purposes of this discussion, I am applying it to the struggle of developing one's career.

We all know that our personal and professional development takes a lot of work. It can seem tiring and frustrating at times. This is why tenacity is very important! In the song, we are reminded that we've come a long way, and that while the journey is far from over and certainly not easy, God will not leave us. The key is faith and determination. These two elements will take you a long way. They will allow you to keep a strong, firm grip on your plans so that you can achieve your goal.

E is for Explorative or Examined

Explore through Research: Using tools like a standard internet search engine and sites that provide employer reviews, run searches to find the best companies to work for based on your criteria. Employer review websites are great because they provide real company data (salaries, numbers of employees, location, etc), and they give access to peer reviews. Other resources that are great tools for research include association websites, online salary calculators, company websites, people who work in industries or companies of interest, and your local library.

Informational interviews are another great way to research a company or a department. I am a huge fan of informational interviews because their benefits are multi-fold. Here a few benefits:

- Creates a Networking opportunity: By requesting an informational interview, you are networking! You are making new contacts and establishing a rapport with people in the industry or company in which you would like to be employed.

- Establishes interest: Informational Interviews let the employers know that you are interested.

- Provides information: Informational interviews give you the opportunity to learn more about the company, department, and available positions. They also give you access to unadvertised or hidden job opportunities.

Throughout my career, I have had several informational interviews. Each one proved to be beneficial, in one way or another. Some have solidified my interest in a company or position. Others have shown me that the company or department would not have been a good fit for me, based on my own career development wants and needs. I have had informational interviews lead to job opportunities.

G is for God-Centered

Let's Reflect. We spent Chapter 3 talking about this characteristic, but as we review the other characteristics, I want to be sure that we don't lose sight of this one, or forget its power. While the nine characteristics need to work together for a successful career development strategy, G is for God-Centered is the most important. It should be done before you begin your strategy, as well as throughout. Proverbs 16: 1-4 is an excellent reminder to us.

1 To humans belong the plans of the heart, but from the Lord comes the proper answer of the tongue. 2 All a person's ways seem pure to them, but motives are weighed by the Lord. 3 Commit to the Lord whatever you do, and he will establish your plans. 4 The Lord works out everything to its proper end. . . . (Proverbs 16: 1-4 NIV)

We should not move by our own desires in decision-making, but instead, we should seek God's will. Jesus gave us the model prayer, in which he asked that His Father's will be done. We should do the same. If we demonstrate our faith and submit to His will, our plans in alignment with His Holy Will, will come to fruition.

I is for Integrity-Guided:

Over the course of my career, in corporate and in education, I've been in the position to recruit, screen, and select candidates for various positions. There is one candidate that I will never forget. Let's call her "Dana" for purposes of this example:

On paper, Dana was amazing! Her resume was perfect. She had the exact experience we were seeking, and I knew that if her in-person interview was as amazing as her credentials, she would be our choice to fill the position.

I was immediately impressed. She interviewed beautifully. She was personable, descriptive, articulate. Her letters of reference backed up the experience she advertised on her resume, and she offered professional references to provide further proof of her abilities.

I checked her references, and invited her back for a second interview to meet my manager. My manager was also impressed by Dana's resume and references. The one thing that stood out for my boss was the education that Dana listed on her resume and application. On her resume, she had indicated that she graduated from a small college in the Northwest. Oddly enough, my boss had also attended the college that Dana had listed, and I was sure that would seal the deal.

The second interview went well and my boss was prepared to offer Dana the position. During a casual chat on our way back to the elevator, my boss asked Dana about her experiences in college. She was unable to clearly answer any questions about her college experience. Her cool, calm, and confident demeanor changed. She was clearly uncomfortable and notably less articulate. That immediately raised red flags for us.

We later learned that Dana had indeed attended the university, but only for one semester. She had not graduated from the school as she indicated on her resume. My boss and I were very disappointed. Her experience landed her the interview, but one lie on her resume cost her the job offer!

As tempting as it may be to fudge your experience or education on your resume or during the interview process, <u>never</u> do this. Honesty is the absolute best way to gain and maintain employment. In addition, honesty brings about personal peace and contentment. When you are honest, you never have to worry about keeping up with the deception, or the lie potentially catching up to you.

Even though I used the above example of Dana's lie on her resume, the "I is for Integrity-Guided" characteristic is not just about honesty during the recruitment or interview process. It is about having and demonstrating strong moral principles throughout your career. Your integrity and honor are so valuable. Once people trust you, the sky is the limit.

Because I've consistently demonstrated strong moral character, employers and clients have repeatedly entrusted me with confidential information, responsibilities and opportunities that others have been denied.

C is for Conviction-powered:
Many people will define conviction as a strong belief. While this is true, it is only part of it. Your convictions are much more than your beliefs. Convictions are the values that motivate us and drive our conduct. Convictions should be the basis of our decision-making. We can develop our convictions by consistently reading the word and attending a church in which we are learning and growing.

As Christians, we want to be sure that the job that we do is in alignment with God's Holy will for us. Instead of worrying about self-satisfaction, let's focus on powering our career development with our convictions. Living by our convictions can empower and protect us during difficult or frustrating times. . . especially in our career development.

11 Put on the full armor of God, so that you can take your stand against the devil's schemes. 12 For our struggle is not against flesh and blood, but against the rulers, against the authorities, against the powers of this dark world and against the spiritual forces of evil in the heavenly realms. 13 Therefore put on the full armor of God, so that when the day of evil comes, you may be able to stand your ground, and after you have done everything, to stand. (Ephesians 6:11-13 NIV)

CHAPTER 6
YOUR INDIVIDUAL SUCCESS PLAN (ISP)

Now that we have covered the characteristics of a successful career development strategy, let's talk about adding some structure and more clearly defining our career development strategy. In this chapter, I will cover the following:

- some things you should consider when creating your plan for success, and
- how to create your ISP.

But first, let us take a quick look at the steps to a successful career strategy:

1) Seek God first and throughout the process

2) Complete a self-assessment

3) Explore/Research careers

4) Develop your ISP

5) Implement

I've illustrated the steps in the diagram on the next page.

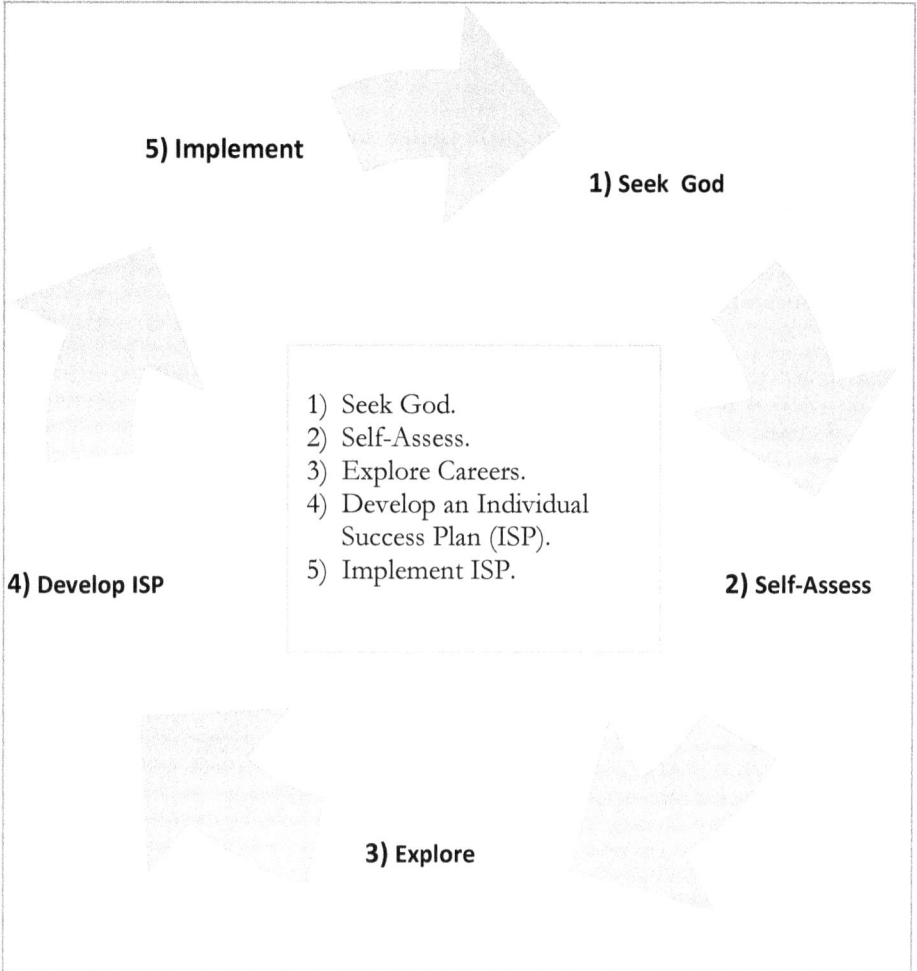

5) Implement

1) Seek God

1) Seek God.
2) Self-Assess.
3) Explore Careers.
4) Develop an Individual
   Success Plan (ISP).
5) Implement ISP.

4) Develop ISP

2) Self-Assess

3) Explore

Defining Career Success:

In Chapter 1, we explored success as it relates to our personal and professional lives. Because our professional lives intersect our personal lives, we need to create an all encompassing picture of what success looks like for you. In that chapter, I encouraged you to consider success for the various areas of your life using the success factor model. The model illustrated the idea, but I explained that for each of us the model could appear differently.

When defining career success, be sure to consider the following:

1) **Values:** Your values are those things that guide what is important in your life. They define the beliefs and ideas by which you live. Values lie at your foundation. As such, they are at the core of developing one's definition of career success. What do you value most? What companies or jobs reflect/support your values? As you work to define "career success", be sure to consider if your definition incorporates your values.

2) **Talents and Strengths:** Understanding your talents and strengths is a key component of defining career success. Building on your strengths will allow you to master your craft, and put you in a more profitable position as you create your path to career success. What types of roles would best utilize your talents, strengths, knowledge, skills, and abilities?

3) **Passion:** Find your passion. Live your purpose. Sometimes embarking on a career that allows you to live according to your purpose is scary and uncomfortable, as it may take you outside of our comfort zone. What is your purpose? What are you passionate about? Is it important for you to have a career that allows you to live your purpose?

4) **Money:** Let's face it: money is important. We may try to downplay its importance in our lives, but the fact is we all need money for the minimal resources needed to sustain our basic physiological needs, such as shelter, food, and clothing. But many of us have a particular lifestyle that we wish to live. We may want to live in a certain neighborhood, drive a particular type of car, eat at our favorite restaurants, etc. We will need money in order to achieve and maintain that lifestyle. What are your Financial Needs/ Desires?

Your ISP

Now that you understand the essential characteristics to a successful career development strategy and the associated steps, it is time to learn how to create an ISP. Creating the plan is easy; however, when done correctly, it should take some time to design. Let's revisit the success factor model that I shared in Chapter 1:

Job
satisfaction

Autonomy
(Independence)

Economic
status

Freedom   **Success**   Recognition

Happiness

Work-Life
balance

Family

When creating your plan, you will consider the exercise you did in Chapter 1, in which you answered a series of questions for each factor.

Individual Success Plan

Consider the factors from Chapter 1 when creating your plan. In this section, I will explain the components of the ISP. In the Appendix of this book, there is a worksheet template that you can use to build your ISP.

1) Personal Vision Statement
Create a three sentence statement which defines your vision for your life.

2) Long Term Goal Statement
In 5 years, where do you see yourself? Using the tips I've provided, create a long-term goal statement in sentence structure for each of the following. Your goal statement should be written in very specific, clear language; include measurable outcomes; have clearly defined action associated with each goal, and attainable.

- **Career:** Where? What position? Salary? Work/Life Balance? Recognition? Etc.

- **Money:** Salary? Investments? Savings? 401k? Other sources of income?

- **Family:** What will your family structure look like? Schooling for children (college, private school, etc.)? Other family considerations?

- **Health:** How will you improve your health or maintain current healthy habits?

- **Vacation/** **Leisure:** Family vacations? "Me" time? Relaxation?

- **Happiness:** What will make you happy? What will happiness look like?

3) *Identify Barriers and Threats to Achieving Your Goal*

When creating an ISP, we must be 100% honest with ourselves. Once the Long-Term Goal is identified, it is time to consider all of the things both internal and external that could get in the way of each of the goals being achieved. Consider personal habits; existing knowledge, skills, and abilities, and outside forces that could impact your ability to achieve success.

4) *Short- Term Goal Statement*

In one year's time, what are you going to do to advance your goal and what are you going to do to overcome the barrier or threat identified above? For example, if you identified "lack of education" as a barrier, a short-term goal could be to enroll in school or certificate program. In this section, consider knowledge, skills, and abilities that need to be developed in order to achieve your long term goal.

Create a short-term goal statement that states what your short term goal to be accomplished in one year will be?

- **Career**
- **Money**
- **Family**
- **Health**
- **Vacation/Leisure**
- **Happiness**

5) *Action Plan/ To-Do List*

Once you have identified your short and long term goals, it is time to create your plan for action. What can you commit to doing daily to get you closer to your short term goal? Weekly?

Consider the following:
- identify and analyze the gap: compare your actual knowledge, skills, and abilities with what is needed for the position. Develop a to-do list to close the gap.

- establishing target dates for the various steps within each goal, and

- what you are going to do each day and each week to get you one step closer to the goal.

6) *ISP Report Card / Monthly Status Check!*

Accountability is key! In order for this plan to work, you must hold yourself accountable for results. To do this, I suggest setting up a regular schedule once per month (at minimum) to review your progress. I also strongly suggest finding an accountability partner – someone who will help to hold you accountable for your progress. This should be someone you trust and can depend on to be honest and direct with you!

- **How Often?**
- **How will you measure progress success or failure?**

CHAPTER 7
MARKETING YOU 101

Alexandria finished talking, and shifted in her seat while staring anxiously across the desk at Mr. Smith, the Hiring Manager. Mr. Smith was looking over her resume again. The silence was very uncomfortable for Alexandria, as she watched his eyes moving slowly across the page. "What is he thinking?," she wondered. He had just asked her the standard "Tell me about yourself" question. She knew her answer was a bit unorganized and long-winded. She wasn't at all confident in her answer. As she sat there in silence, she thought of things she should have said, but she didn't want to start talking again. In fact, she was concerned that she may have lost his attention with her rambling answer.

Now that we have covered the characteristics of an effective career development strategy and the steps to implementing an ISP, it is time to explore self-marketing.

Go Beyond the Plan. . . . Be the Brand!

Think about everyday products: beverages, shoes, fast food, toilet paper, car insurance. Then think about the branding that various companies use to market their products: logos, slogans, cute mascots. Their brand is their identity; it is what differentiates them from other companies.

Maybe you've never considered this before, but you also have a brand. It is that combination of skills, experiences, and attitudinal qualities that sets you apart from others. It is this combination that you can "package" and market, as you continue along your journey to professional development. Determine the message you want to send, and demonstrate it!

Throughout your career, you will have to market yourself effectively.

Whether you are looking for a job, simply trying to maintain your job, or seeking a raise or promotion, the image that you project is very important.

As much as I tell my 8-year-old daughter that what others think is unimportant, the truth is that in our career development, the perception of others does matter. Let me explain: If you are seeking a promotion to a management position, it is important that you are perceived as a leader or as someone with leadership potential. If the decision makers cannot envision you as someone capable of managing others, your chances of moving into a management position are probably slim! So, the idea here, is to ensure that the decision makers and those with influence on the decision-makers can see you in the position you are seeking.

I am not encouraging you to be manipulative. Instead, I am suggesting that you identify the skill set, qualities, and attitudes essential to the position where you want to be, and demonstrate those skills and qualities. Be able to "talk the talk" and "walk the walk".

In interview settings, clearly articulate your worth and provide concrete examples of experiences you have that meet the employer's needs. If you do not have those skills yet, don't worry! Just make sure they are listed in your ISP as skills you need to develop, and make sure you work on them!

Resuscitate Your Pitch with the CPR Approach

In this chapter's opening example, Alexandria struggled with the question "Tell me about yourself." This is a question that is typically asked in one form or another during an interview. So make sure you are prepared for it! As you are developing your personal brand, you have to be able to sell yourself. In other words, you need a commercial. When someone asks "Why should I hire you?" or "What do you do?", you should be ready with your CPR Personal Branding Pitch. CPR stands for Clear, Persuasive, and Relevant:

- **Clear:** easy to follow, direct.
- **Persuasive:** contains language that persuades them to want to learn more about you,
- **Relevant:** with concrete examples that can be directly tied to the desired qualifications for the position

Self-Marketing Tips

As you embark on this journey to career success, there are some important tips to remember:

1) **Create a Powerful Resume and Cover Letter:** In many cases, your resume and cover letter are your first introduction to a company. Make sure your first impression is powerful and memorable.

2) **Consistent Messaging:** Think about how companies advertise. Most repeat a single, consistent message about their products or services.

   Your cover letter, resume, interview answers, and online networking profiles should all have consistent information. Make sure that when you update information, it is updated across all platforms.

3) **Prepare for Challenges:** Let's be honest. There may be things about your experience, education, or skills that others may view as deficits. The key to a successful self-marketing strategy is not to ignore the possible perception. Instead you must prepare for it. How? It is very simple. By anticipating real or perceived short-comings, you can create powerful, hard-hitting responses to any objection.

4) **Practice Your CPR Personal Branding Pitch.** While you do not have to know it word for word, it is imperative that you can deliver the information succinctly and effectively. Avoid extended pauses and the use of unnecessary filler sounds, words, and phrases. Some common fillers to avoid are:

   uh, um, literally, basically,
   actually, you know, I believe.

5) **Communicate Your Brand Through Networking:** Network! Network! Network! Networking is a productive way to further your career development efforts. Get in front of the right people and be

ready to deliver your winning CPR personal branding statement. Today's technology has made connecting with the right people incredibly simple. There are so many sites and resources available that allow you to identify hiring managers, and make direct contact.

Use online professional networking sites and mobile apps, attend networking events, and request informational interviews.

6) **Showcase Your Accomplishments:** It is not boastful when you promote your accomplishments as part of the career development process. Be proud and confident, and share your accomplishments with the decision makers and influencers. You can showcase in person using a portfolio, and verbally sharing your experiences and successes. You can showcase remotely via social media, website, blog, and electronic letters of recommendation.

CHAPTER 8
ENDLESS POSSIBILITIES!

The process of career development can be a lifelong journey. We are always growing, learning, and developing. Each day, there is something new and wonderful to learn and understand --- if we are willing to open our minds. The possibilities for growth and development are endless.

Success is within your reach. Reading this book is only the beginning for you. With a well-thought-out plan, a God-centered strategy, dedication to the process, and your willingness to take consistent, deliberate action toward realistic goals, you can achieve.

Do not be discouraged by failure or "no's". This is not easy, but try to view closed doors as a re-routed opportunity, a detoured breakthrough. Many times, a door may be closed so that God's purpose for your life can be manifested.

I used to let "No" discourage me until I realized that what I perceived as rejection was simply redirecting me to greater possibilities for my life. I have seen evidence of this repeatedly in my life.

God is our Father, and He wants the very best for His children. He wants us to be happy and to take refuge in Him! He wants us to lean and depend on Him. Sometimes, we may not understand the how, what, where, and why; but we must continue to have faith in Him, knowing that He will guide us and position us in the right place for our purpose.

> 5 Trust in the LORD with all your heart and lean not on your own understanding; 6 in all your ways acknowledge him, and he will make your paths straight. (Proverbs 3:5-6

Let us pray:

Heavenly Father, we come before you in the name of your loving Son, Jesus --- grateful for all that you have done in our personal and professional lives thus far. We are thankful for every triumph and every failure, for every yes and for every no, for every roadblock and every detour – because we know that each experience presents a new opportunity for growth. We know that the very best is yet to come, and so we thank you right now for what you are going to do in our lives.

As we embark on a new approach to our career development, centered on You, we ask for your guidance. Please bless the work of our hands. Lord, order our steps according to your perfect will. Give us grace as we stand before the decision-makers and hiring managers, Heavenly Father.

We ask you to help us maintain an integrity-driven and conviction-powered career development strategy. Please strengthen our faith and renew our strength, as we face new obstacles and barriers each day. We know that all things are possible through You. There is nothing too hard for You, God.

You are our provider, our helper, our healer, our shepherd. You are our creator, our Lord and master! You are our Most High God, sovereign over all. You are our omnipresent, omnipotent, omniscient God!

Please continue to meet our needs according to your riches in Glory. We lift this prayer in the precious name of your Son and our Savior, Jesus Christ.

Amen.

APPENDIX: ADDITIONAL RESOURCES

In Chapter 2, I discussed defining success using the Success Factors Map; and in Chapter 6, I discussed creating an Individual Success Plan (ISP). You can use the pages that follow to develop your personal definition of success and create your own ISP.

Please refer back to Chapters 2 and 6 for guidelines, instructions, and examples.

Remember, your definition of success and your ISP should be very detailed and specific. You may find that the templates on the following pages do not provide you with enough room. Feel free to reproduce or re-create the forms for personal use.

DEFINING SUCCESS

Now it's time for you to define success, using the model I discussed in Chapter 1:

1) Using the Success Factor map below, fill in the factors that are relevant to you. Here is a list of the factors that we used in Chapter 1:

- job satisfaction
- work-life balance
- recognition
- finances
- position/title

- economic status
- independence
- freedom
- happiness
- family

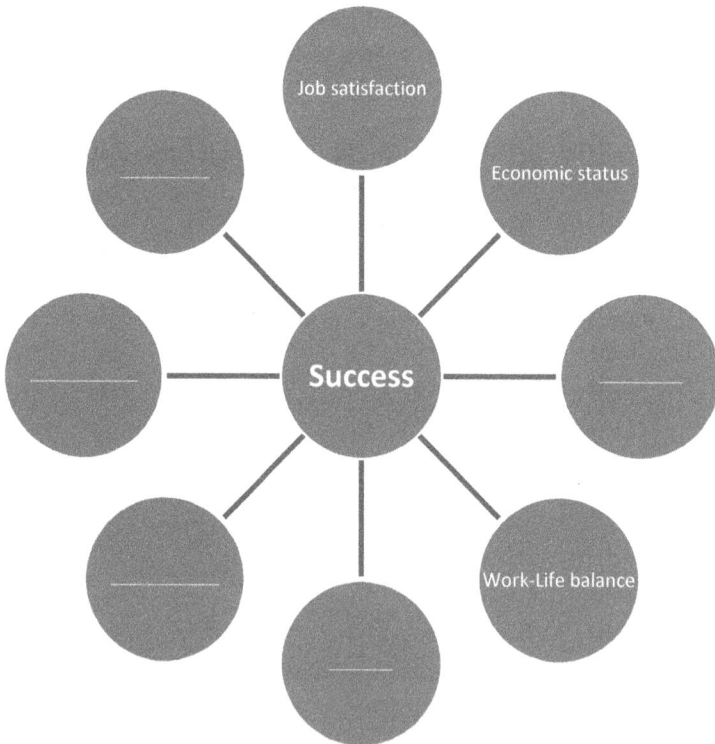

Be STRATEGIC

Success Factor:

What does success look like in terms of _____?

```



```

On a scale of **1-10**, how important is _____ to me in my overall view of Success? Why?

```



```

What steps will I take to achieve _____?

```



```

What can I do today to get me one step closer to _____ ?

```



```

What other factors are impacted by _____?

```



```

ISP: Consider the factors from Chapter 1 when creating your plan:

1) Personal Vision Statement

Create a three sentence statement which defines your vision for your life:

2) Long Term Goal Statement (5 Years)

- **Career:**

- **Money:**

- **Family:**

- **Health:**

- **Vacation/ Leisure:**

- **Happiness:**

3) *Identify Barriers and Threats to Achieving Your Goal*

4) *Short- Term Goal Statement*

- **Career:**

- **Money:**

- **Family:**

- **Health:**

- **Vacation/ Leisure:**

- **Happiness:**

5) *Action Plan/ To-Do List*

6) *ISP Report Card / Regular Status Check!*

Establish a schedule and an accountability plan for ensuring that you are on target to reach your short- and long-term goals.

ABOUT THE AUTHOR

Kimberly Ferguson is a professional development trainer, speaker, and coach. Passionate about helping others grow and develop professionally, she has the demonstrated ability to engage and motivate learners. Professionally, she has more than 16 years combined experience in the areas of Training, Education, Marketing, Business Development, and Management.

Kimberly has worked for public, private, start-up, non-profit companies, as well as in Secondary and Higher Education. Her experience spans the training and presenting gamut.

In addition, Kimberly is a certified teacher. An experienced Career Development instructor, she designed and assisted in the implementation of a successful Career Development initiative for a county-wide alternative high school program. She has also designed and implemented successful professional development programs for adults for non-profit, city, state, and private agencies.

Through her company, K-Ferg Training, Kimberly provides customized training solutions and coaching for a number of clients.

Kimberly and her husband, Dewey, currently reside in New Jersey with their two beautiful daughters.

www.ingramcontent.com/pod-product-compliance
Lightning Source LLC
Chambersburg PA
CBHW060051050426
42448CB00011B/2401